. . . AND THEN SOME

GAGE | [2] SHE SPOKE VOLUMES

SHE SPOKE VOLUMES

... AND THEN SOME

… AND THEN SOME

SHE SPOKE VOLUMES
. . . AND THEN SOME

Onedia N. Gage, Ph. D.

… AND THEN SOME

GAGE | [6] SHE SPOKE VOLUMES

DEDICATION

For those who have witnessed these words

For those who have endured these words

For those who have repeated these words

For those who wish I would not repeat these words

For those who are inspired by these words

For those who are motivated by these words

For those who need these words,

Here they are . . . finally!

...AND THEN SOME

SCRIPTURES

May these words of my mouth ad this meditation of my heart be pleasing in Your sight, Lord, my Rock and my Redeemer

Psalm 19:14 (NIV)

For gaining wisdom and instruction; for understanding words of insight;

Proverbs 1:2 (NIV)

Love extravagantly.

1 Corinthians 13:13 (MSG)

... AND THEN SOME

LIBRARY OF CONGRESS

She Spokes Volumes
. . . And Then Some

All Rights Reserved © 2018
Rev. Onedia N. Gage

No part of this of book may be reproduced or transmitted in
Any form or by any means, graphic, electronic, or mechanical,
Including photocopying, recording, taping, or by any
Information storage or retrieval system, without the
Permission in writing from the publisher.

Purple Ink, Inc. Press

For Information:
Purple Ink, Inc.
P O Box 300113
Houston, TX 77230

www.purpleink.net ♦ www.onediagage.com

publish@purpleink.net ♦ onediagage@onediagage.com

ISBN:

978-1-939119-65-0

Printed in United States

SHE SPOKE VOLUMES

MORE BOOKS BY
ONEDIA N. GAGE, PH. D.

90 Days of Powerful Words: Affirmation and Advice for Girls
Are You Ready for 9th Grade . . . Again? A Family's Guide to Success
As We Grow Together Daily Devotional for Expectant Couples
As We Grow Together Prayer Journal for Expectant Couples
As We Grow Together Bible Study: Her Workbook
As We Grow Together Bible Study: His Workbook
The Best 40 Days of My Life: A Journey of Spiritual Renewal
The Blue Print: Poetry for the Soul
From Fat to Fit in 90 Days: A Fitness Journal
From Two to One: The Notebook for the Christian Couple
Hannah's Voice: Powerful Lessons in Prayer
Her Story The Legacy of Her Fight: The Bible Study
Her Story The Legacy of Her Fight: The Devotional
Her Story The Legacy of Her Fight: The Legacy Journal
Her Story The Legacy of Her Fight: Prayers and Journal
ILY! A Mother Daughter Relationship Workbook
In Her Own Words: Notebook for the Christian Woman
In Purple Ink: Poetry for the Spirit
Intensive Couples Retreat: Her Workbook
Intensive Couples Retreat: His Workbook
Living A Whole Life: Sermons Which Provide, Prompt, and Promote Life
Love Letters to God from a Teenage Girl
The Measure of a Woman: The Details of Her Soul
The Notebook: For Me, About Me, By Me
The Notebook for the Christian Teen
On This Journey Daily Devotional for Young People
On This Journey Prayer Journal for Young People
On This Journey Prayer Journal for Young People, Vol. 2
One Day More Than We Deserve Prayer Journal for the Growing Christian
Promises, Promises: A Christian Novel
Queen in the Making: 30 Week Bible Study for Teen Girls

. . . AND THEN SOME[11] | GAGE

. . . AND THEN SOME

Six Months of Solitude: The Sanctity of Singleness Notebook
Six Months of Solitude: The Sanctity of Singleness Prayers and Journal
Tools for These Times: Timely Sermons for Uncertain Times
With An Anointed Voice: The Power of Prayer
Yielded and Submitted: A Woman's Journey for a Life Dedicated to God
Yielded and Submitted: A Woman's Journey for a Life Dedicated to God An Intimate Study
Yielded and Submitted: A Woman's Journey for a Life Dedicated to God Prayers and Journal

SHE SPOKE VOLUMES

DEAR GOD,

Well Father, I am here. I only have myself, Your creation to offer back to You. I pray your blessings over my wisdom for my future and what you have for me. I do not want to disappoint You, although every day I am close or perfect at doing it. Please help me with that.

I am exercising all of the faith that I have each word, each paragraph, each page, and each book. I am waiting on Your solution. God, I am in a special place. One where only You and I occupy.

I am praying that I have pleased You in this book. I keep praying that I will please You with my faith.

Lord, I would whine and wish but I am not. Just give Me what You have planned according Your will. I love You and just want You to be pleased with me.

Thank You for forgiving me of my sins. Thank You for Your abounding love. And Your amazing grace.

I pray that others are blessed with these words. I pray that they grow from my notes.

In Jesus' name, I pray these blessings.

Amen.

Your daughter,

Onedia

. . . AND THEN SOME

GAGE | [14] SHE SPOKE VOLUMES

SHE SPOKE VOLUMES

DEAR READER,

I hope that these words bring you hope and balance, love and resolve. There are many words, which I have spoken or written in several places. I know that you will need time to embrace them all. I am known for my outrageous and outlandish views and those views becoming words. I am authentic, which intimidates others. This is not a moment that goes by that words do not come to mind, and following that thought, those words are easily on paper or out loud.

I pray that they serve you well to encourage, uplift, push, challenge and reflect on your personal life and all that it entails. I am certain that you will use them from time to time, but most importantly, I want to consider the message and how that will propel you forward with your life's mission and vision. I am overwhelmed by what God continues to do in my life. I hope that this is happening in your life as well.

I know that you are ready to grow and to expand for the benefit of you and your life. I hope that this helps you with that journey.

I am hopeful that you are growing and loving, thinking and creating the life that you always dreamed of. I am working daily and diligently on my own and I hope that we are moving forward with zest and zeal. This is a prudent time in your life. A time to strategize and risk that which you usually hold back and exercise the conservative side.

Keep working. Keep pressing. Keep focused. Keep motivated. Keep your wits about you. Keep aiming high. Winning is imminent.

Love in purple,

Onedia N. Gage

... AND THEN SOME

TABLE OF CONTENTS

DEDICATION	7
SCRIPTURE	9
PRAYER	13
LETTER	15
THE WORDS	19
POEM	279
ACKNOWLEDGEMENTS	281
ABOUT THE WORD MASTER	283

. . . AND THEN SOME

GAGE | [18] SHE SPOKE VOLUMES

SHE SPOKE VOLUMES

. . . AND THEN SOME

. . . AND THEN SOME

GAGE | [20] SHE SPOKE VOLUMES

God,
I put YOU in charge of every detail of my life, even the pain I feel in my heart.

. . . AND THEN SOME

Your

decisions

are

based

on

your

past,

with

a

future

in

mind.

Decide wisely.

SHE SPOKE VOLUMES

YOU HAVE GOT TO LOVE A MAN WHO PUTS YOUR SHOES ON FOR YOU!

#SCANDAL

Love like you mean it!!!!

Like it's all you've got!!!!

... AND THEN SOME[23] | GAGE

If I am who I say that I am, then your struggle should move me, should propel me to take action on your behalf, and should provoke a profound compassion that you would have a hard time understanding because no one cares like this. So, do not retreat when my care and love (agape) overwhelms you and seems unrealistic, like I want something in return. Just stand there and let God bless you through me.

When you ask God for help through your struggles, pain and brokenness, you should start to look for the answer around you through persons He will send you. Expect someone to show up, sometimes they don't even know that they are on assignment. They have just what can help you, led to you by God for your recovery and healing and solution.

. . . AND THEN SOME

Even though the connection may not be immediate,

it is still important to make the connection.

The investment is worth it.

IF YOU TRUST LOVE, THEN THE RISK IS WORTHWHILE.

SHE SPOKE VOLUMES

IF YOU WERE GOING TO LOVE ME AND TAKE CARE OF MY HEART,

THEN CERTAINLY YOU WOULD HAVE DONE IT BY NOW.

I don't have any evidence that I have missed anything when I walked away from that relationship.

...AND THEN SOME

AN INSECURE WOMAN WILL WREAK HAVOC ON YOUR LIFE. A SECURE WOMAN WILL PROPEL YOUR LIFE FORWARD WITH INTENSITY, TRAJECTORY, AND PURPOSE. FIGURE OUT HOW TO MAKE HER SECURE. SHE DESERVES IT AND YOU WILL ENJOY THE BENEFITS!!!

HOW ARE YOU GOING TO BE DIFFERENT?

SHE SPOKE VOLUMES

When I speak, what do you hear?

Wherever you are, you are on assignment.

God does not do wild goose chases!!!

...AND THEN SOME

Keeping in mind that change starts with you!

I'm starting with me!!!!

BECAUSE CHANGING ONE LIFE IS NOT ENOUGH, I KEEP DOING IT OVER AND OVER AGAIN!

SHE SPOKE VOLUMES

WHAT IS GOD'S PLAN?
WHAT IS GOD'S WILL?
DON'T MOVE OR QUIT UNTIL YOU KNOW!

...AND THEN SOME

YOU CAN ALWAYS START TODAY WITH BEING HONEST WITH YOURSELF!

YOU KNOW I CAN HEAR YOU . . . .

If I can help you to find your voice, will you let me help you?

SHE SPOKE VOLUMES

I AM A TESTIMONY IN THE MAKING.

———————————————————

... AND THEN SOME[33] | GAGE

... AND THEN SOME

God, You put me here for a reason. I am starving to know exactly what it is right now. But while I wait on You to reveal what I will be doing next, I will sit here and do as much I can to be obedient as You process and prepare me. Thanks for the plans You have for me and I am so glad that they are better than the ones I thought up. Jeremiah 29:11.

SHE SPOKE VOLUMES

It's wise to research your competition before you challenge your competition to a showdown.

SOME THINGS ARE JUST WORTH WORKING FOR.

. . . AND THEN SOME[35] | GAGE

...AND THEN SOME

Love does not cost, but the results are priceless!

Education should be priority.

Costs should not matter!

SHE SPOKE VOLUMES

"He meant what he said, and he said what he meant. An elephant is loyal 100%." Horton hears a Who.

But isn't that what we do? We say what we mean but we are not taken at our word but that's part of our personality. It is who we are.

I'm learning to listen carefully to what the other person says, replay to myself what they said and then understand that that is their truth. I does not need to make sense to me, nor do I have to like it. It means that I decide if I can handle it, I understand that it is not subject to change.

... AND THEN SOME

Vulnerability produces the best version of strength.

IT IS TIME TO EXECUTE THOSE GREAT IDEAS!

PLEASE ABANDON THE ANALYSIS PARALYSIS!

Because of my limitations, not without those limitations, I will succeed.

Even I can't stand in God's way for what He has for me.

YOU JUST BROKE YOUR OWN RULES!

...AND THEN SOME

Loving me the way I deserve and need and desire is not optional. Neither is it for you. Please layout out your road map and I will lay out mine. Give me some time and lessons on the map. I will do all that I can to show up in the right places at the right time for the right reasons so that my love will be completely clear to you. I love you in the most authentic manner you allow. I am working daily to deepen, intensify and magnify our love. I do need your help. I need your TOTAL engagement.

SHE SPOKE VOLUMES

Did the passing of a legend change your attitude and plans and actions?

It should have. Do it now. The impossible. The crazy. The ridiculous. The very things that others have shaken their heads about when you have spoken them out loud.

Do those things now.

Do the things you fear the most first.

... AND THEN SOME

Just because I make this look easy does not mean it is.

SHE SPOKE VOLUMES

Please do not expect my results if you are not willing to duplicate my work and my work ethic.

...AND THEN SOME

I made that mistake because I didn't believe the results of my own homework and research. Trust what you know.

SHE SPOKE VOLUMES

I AM BUILT TO WIN!
I AM FORGIVEN!
I AM EQUIPPED FOR SUCCESS!

... AND THEN SOME

USUALLY I DON'T MIND AND AM WILLING BUT TODAY I JUST NEED SOLUTIONS FOR YOUR PROBLEMS AND MINE. NO NEW ISSUES OR COMPLAINTS ARE BEING RECEIVED AT THIS TIME. THANK YOU.

SHE SPOKE VOLUMES

I DON'T NEED TO BE REMINDED TO LOVE YOU.

I JUST NEED YOU TO BE PRESENT FOR ME TO DO SO.

... AND THEN SOME[47] | GAGE

...AND THEN SOME

I am not sure that I can be any more plain or clear than I already am.

We take for granted far more than what we selectively appreciate.

Love is an option to those who lack foundation. For the rest of us, love is our oxygen.

... AND THEN SOME

Because your stupidity is memorable.

SHE SPOKE VOLUMES

When you have given away your belief, but you kept your pride;
When you have given away your hope, but you are a slave to your fears;
When you have given away your love, but you are driven by your hate;
When you have absconded your faith, but you are holding on to your hurt
and brokenness,

You are not living.

You are in fact the definition of the walking dead we muse about.

Awaken those dead bones and that dry and neglected spirit.

Renew your love and your heart so it can feel free to function.

All of this is done in an outlandish and outrageous manner.

Without limits and fear.

If you could give up the good, then the bad should be even easier.

... AND THEN SOME[51] | GAGE

... AND THEN SOME

I expect you to love me as aggressively as you pursued me.

Our children exist to hold us accountable for our choices and decisions.

. . . AND THEN SOME

I'm not stupid when I treat you better than you deserve. It's who I am. I know that you don't deserve the best of me. The fact is that you know it too.

SHE SPOKE VOLUMES

You got the wrong answer because you asked the wrong question.

IF YOU LOVE SOMEONE,

THEN THEY DESERVE YOU AS AN AUDIENCE.

The greatest rewards come after the biggest risks.

. . . AND THEN SOME[55] | GAGE

...AND THEN SOME

When I really try to love you, will you understand the weight and the depth, height and breadth and content of that love in the manner in which it is presented, with all of my wholeness and fullness? In the authentic, overwhelming presentation that I so often bring, without reservation or regard for the outcome? I'm just asking because I am just trying to get this right. I promise that I want to love you because I want to.

DOES ANYONE ELSE UNDERSTAND WHY PEOPLE CANNOT ANSWER A QUESTION? JUST ANSWER THE QUESTION. I'M NOT GOING TO SAY THE QUESTION IS SIMPLE OR EASY BUT JUST ANSWER THE QUESTION OR OFFER ME THE RESPECT OF MY INTELLIGENCE AND NOT TRY TO AVOID THE QUESTION, ACTING LIKE YOU ANSWERED BUT REALLY TRIED TO CHANGE THE SUBJECT AS IF I WOULDN'T NOTICE ALTHOUGH I PUT PLENTY OF THOUGHT IN THE QUESTION, THUS THE ANSWER IT WOULD PRODUCE!

...AND THEN SOME

The person you love and who loves you should get the best of you and all that you have!

I didn't want to win until someone said I couldn't.

. . . AND THEN SOME

People who want to understand the path of the people who lead them will find out what their leaders are reading.

Leaders, what are you reading? Are you sharing what you are reading? Are you teaching the why? Are you really building capacity?

Do they practice leading with you in the room? Or do you have to hear about it? If you are in the room, and then offer valuable feedback.

That is building capacity.

SHE SPOKE VOLUMES

IT'S AMAZING THAT PEOPLE ONLY HAVE THE COURAGE TO DO SOME THINGS WHEN YOU ARE NOT PRESENT.

When you consider who you really are, how would you grade yourself? Do you curve your grade and what is that based on? Do you offer others that same allowance? When you are hold others accountable, are the standards the same?

... AND THEN SOME

HIGH HEELS MAKE YOU BEHAVE BETTER!

SHE SPOKE VOLUMES

I praise the Lord for broken yokes!

. . . AND THEN SOME

> I'M NOT TO HOLDING YOU ACCOUNTABLE FOR SOMETHING YOU DO NOT KNOW AND FOR WHICH YOU SHOULD NOT BE ACCOUNTABLE.

SHE SPOKE VOLUMES

Making up this legacy from scratch; one day at a time.

. . . AND THEN SOME

When you realize that your life is not your own, but that you are a part of something larger, something global, then a change in you is required; action is expected; behavior is important.

MY PRAYERS ARE DEDICATED TO THOSE FAMILIES AND FRIENDS WHO LOST LOVED ONES IN THE SEPTEMBER 11ᵀᴴ ATTACKS.

WE ARE STILL PRAYING FOR YOU!

...AND THEN SOME

I'm not apologizing for having standards or for the standards that I have.

All decisions you make will determine whether you are successful or not. When you make a decision, which could result in a failure, please be prepared to fail without excuse or blame.

. . . AND THEN SOME

There are statements which you will make with the best of intentions to encourage others that you yourself don't believe and cannot personally carry out. When you make statements, which push others toward excellence, it's not too late to follow that fire you started.

SHE SPOKE VOLUMES

Don't expect greatness if you have not done any work.

... AND THEN SOME

I want to add that it's not healthy to keep that hurt harbored in your heart and mind. If he hurt you with those words, then you have some decisions to make. One, you can walk away hoping that the next man won't repeat what he did. Two, you can help him grow so that he never does it again. Forgive him. Stop keeping count of what he did. Love does not do that. 1 Corinthians 13. Thirdly, when he does grow beyond stop holding him hostage for what he did umpteen years ago.

If you can't let that moment go, then let him go. Both of you deserve to be loved completely and wholly, and holistically. If you can't, then leave. Your heart should be free and light, so love can flow through it easily. If it's not, then make the necessary adjustments immediately.

I know that we go through a lot, but we should not have to relive our worst moments on a regular basis. You have to participate in your healing. You have to want to 'walk' again.

SHE SPOKE VOLUMES

MARRIAGE IS A FULL-TIME JOB WITH NO RESIGNATION CLAUSE AND NO TWO WEEKS NOTICES ALLOWED.

... AND THEN SOME

I vow to love you fiercely and extravagantly!

I'm all in.

Without reservation.

SHE SPOKE VOLUMES

Because of my love for Him is how I boldly can love "him."

The relationships are paralleled.

The difference between a relationship and a lifetime is the measure of the intensity of the love. Most won't ever consider being 'all in' because the escape route is established before the commitment is ever presented.

The bar is high.

Reaching it is not hard. Maintenance is daily work.

Prayer is required.

. . . AND THEN SOME

THE WORLD IS NOT SET UP TO RECEIVE ME.

I'm apologizing in advance for my determination which you have defined as offensive, which has caused you to respond defensively. I also want to remind you to look at my heart. Seek to understand why I'm going to move at this speed and with this determination. I also invite you to come with me.

... AND THEN SOME

I CAN'T THANK GOD ENOUGH!

SHE SPOKE VOLUMES

You said quite a few words but, in reality what you said lacked the message you were trying to send. It sounded good, but you didn't say anything! I still need an explanation and I still have several questions. Next time just give me the bottom line with the facts.

Haters have always been here and are not new.

Genesis 37:1-11.

... AND THEN SOME

SOMETIMES THE ANSWER TO SOMEONE'S PRAYER IS YOU!

SHE SPOKE VOLUMES

I am who I say that I am. I keep my word first to myself then to others. I am true to myself and to others as allowed.

If you see otherwise, be sure to share.

...AND THEN SOME

I do sin however, because of my calling, I cannot live there. I am restricted to certain things because of the calling on my life. Because of that same calling, I'm privileged immensely in other areas. I have a request that I hope God honors but if He doesn't, I'm still going to be faithful to Him, His word, and His will. I love you all for praying for me in this season.

JUST FOR THE RECORD, IF SOMEONE ELSE IS TAKING CARE OF IT, IT DOES NOT BELONG TO YOU.

SHE SPOKE VOLUMES

It's hard to understand that what you asked God for is at the end of the valley you are in. Stay the course believing God is keeping you in the valley designed to help you to handle your victory.

My expectations are too high, too much and too personal. My accountability is too overwhelming. Is that what I heard you say?

Just a question of clarity.

CALL TO ACTION DURING THIS POLITICAL SEASON: (1) Pray - comprehensively, intentionally and under the will of God. (2) Share Jesus - this is the believer's CALL TO ACTION. (3) Loving extravagantly - the power of the love that has been given to you. It's not our love to hold on to and dole out as we see fit but it's God's love that is to be given out extravagantly.

> **ALL THAT I'M ASKING IS FOR YOU TO DO WHAT YOU SAY YOU WILL, BE YOURSELF, AND BE HONEST, AT LEAST WITH YOURSELF. I KNOW THAT IS ASKING A LOT. BUT IF NOT, DO THIS: STOP ADVERTISING FALSELY AND STOP SENDING YOUR UNPREPARED REPRESENTATIVE!**

... AND THEN SOME

NOT ONE DAY IS PROMISED TO US. DO THE BEST YOU CAN TO MAKE EACH ONE COUNT.

My purpose includes producing and requiring excellence everywhere I am placed.

. . . AND THEN SOME

"You want to be close to your Creator, mostly because He loves you and your closeness demonstrates the reciprocity of your love."

-Excerpt from Queen in the Making: 30 Week Bible Study for Teen Girls.

SHE SPOKE VOLUMES

> *"If you can love me through my storms, then you can stay. If not, please leave now. I am not sure when the rain will stop nor how much damage will be done. I do not want to think you will be here when all is done."*

. . . AND THEN SOME

I'm not sure why I let myself get so invested. Only to be disappointed.

GAGE | [90] SHE SPOKE VOLUMES

SHE SPOKE VOLUMES

> **I had a conversation today about being a better Christian versus being a good friend. We decided to be a better Christian to our friends.**

...AND THEN SOME

IS THAT WHAT YOUR BIBLE SAYS?

YES, THAT RAIN YOU HEAR OUTSIDE IS REAL.

LIKEWISE, THAT RAIN YOU HEAR INSIDE IS REAL TOO.

. . . AND THEN SOME

The reason that people do not share hundreds of details about themselves and their past is because of the guaranteed judgement you will render about their past. Do not get mad about what they have not shared with you because you will judge them about things that have happened to them that were not even in their control.

SHE SPOKE VOLUMES

I JUST HATE TO HEAR PEOPLE JUST BLATANTLY LIE!

. . . AND THEN SOME[95] | GAGE

. . . AND THEN SOME

Don't be lukewarm!!!!

SHE SPOKE VOLUMES

In competition, your opponent has to view you as a threat.

Otherwise, it's not a competition.

... AND THEN SOME[97] | GAGE

. . . AND THEN SOME

What do you do when realize you are on center stage?

But you didn't know your seat was the stage.

SHE SPOKE VOLUMES

Please

    GO

        OUT OF

            YOUR

                WAY

                    TO

                        AVOID

                            INSULTING

                                MY

                                    INTELLIGENCE.

. . . AND THEN SOME[99] | GAGE

. . . AND THEN SOME

God has to do a lot to keep me out of enemy territory.

I keep trying to go toward enemy territory.

And I keep inviting enemy territory to me.

I make God's job so hard.

SHE SPOKE VOLUMES

We

take

much

more

than

we

should

for

granted.

. . . AND THEN SOME[101] | GAGE

. . . AND THEN SOME

IS IT WORTH THE EFFORT?
IF NOT, JUST WALK AWAY.

SHE SPOKE VOLUMES

Life is too short to quit!

There is no reward for quitting.

There is only drive and determination for the tasks ahead.

Don't ever give up.

... AND THEN SOME

Life teaches lots of lessons.

We have the opportunity to make life work with those lessons.

Don't cut yourself short by ignoring the lessons.

SHE SPOKE VOLUMES

Think big!
DO BIG!!!!

. . . AND THEN SOME

There is a time to talk and there is a time to do.

There is a time to stop talking to people who do not do so that you can DO.

DON'T SPEND SO MUCH TIME ON YOUR PAST THAT YOU MISS YOUR PRESENT, AND STILL END UP WITHOUT A FUTURE. YOU CANNOT BE SUCCESSFUL IF YOU ARE LOOKING FOR YOUR PAST TO REDEEM YOUR FUTURE.

...AND THEN SOME

Sometimes you have to stop so you can win!

SHE SPOKE VOLUMES

She

invited

him

to

love

her,

but he refused.

... AND THEN SOME[109] | GAGE

. . . AND THEN SOME

What do you do when your son says, "Mommy, I thought I was your favorite movie?"

SHE SPOKE VOLUMES

WHY DO PEOPLE HAVE TO BEG YOU TO HELP YOU? NOBODY SHOULD WANT SOMETHING FOR YOU MORE THAN YOU WANT IT FOR YOURSELF.

...AND THEN SOME

When you want to say ALL that is on

your heart and mind,

but you just don't.

SHE SPOKE VOLUMES

Surrendering to God means telling your whole true story—not some 'modified, make you look better, trying to hide your obvious pain beneath hair and makeup (whether yours naturally or purchased), you can't even remember the story you told' version of the truth you tell because you cannot hear your own truth out loud.

From the newest in the collection, ***Hannah's Voice: The Power of Prayer***

. . . AND THEN SOME

Is your mate equipped to be successful in a relationship with you?

Do they know the pitfalls, the minefields, the rules, the regulations, the requirements, and the reasons to celebrate?

If not, why not? If not, when will you equip that mate?

They need your help to be successful.

Help them to win your heart, keep you happy, keep you satisfied, and support your dreams, desires, and efforts.

Help them to be successful.

You liked them enough to love them.

Help them.

Don't be that person who won't help them but will totally invest in the next person.

SHE SPOKE VOLUMES

My name is Onedia N. Gage and I am a Christian and I love Jesus Christ. Despite the fact that I'm human and I fail every day, I believe that Jesus Christ is the Son of God, was crucified on a cross, died for my sins and rose again on the third day to give me salvation. Besides, He loves me dearly, and forgives my sins. His love knows no end and nothing can separate me from His love. I would like to testify of His mercy & grace which are new every morning for me! Ephesians 3:14-21

. . . AND THEN SOME

After

your

personal

definition

of

love

is

announced,

how

do

you

measure

that

love?

SHE SPOKE VOLUMES

ONE OF THE MOST POWERFUL THINGS YOU CAN DO IS WALK AWAY

...FROM A MAN,

FROM A POSITION,

FROM MONEY.

JUST WALK AWAY.

... AND THEN SOME

When you say you love someone, you stay and stand for them for as long as it takes. Through each storm and each dream, you love them.

Through it all!

SHE SPOKE VOLUMES

If you make it too difficult to be in a relationship with you, then the other person may decide to quit.

#onnotice #nonotice

... AND THEN SOME[119] | GAGE

The only Man that loves me unconditionally, listens to my every word, meets my every need, and never interrupts me when I speak is God.

Sometimes we start with the wrong information.

What we should say first, we don't.

What is the most important, we leave off.

. . . AND THEN SOME

When you pick a fight, pick one which leads you to loving another person greater than you ever thought possible, better than they think they deserve, and more extravagantly than is even reasonable. Life is too short for anything else. You deserved to be loved at that level and you deserve to be loved at that same level of extravagance!

SHE SPOKE VOLUMES

Loving out loud requires a lot of courage.

. . . AND THEN SOME[123] | GAGE

... AND THEN SOME

REINVENT YOURSELF!

SHE SPOKE VOLUMES

I only write the important stuff in purple ink.

. . . AND THEN SOME

Please stop self-sabotage.

It's counter-productive and unattractive!

SHE SPOKE VOLUMES

THE KEY TO MOTIVATING SOMEONE IS MEETING THEIR DEEPEST NEED!

... AND THEN SOME

I'm wishing for my first love, while my First Love is beckoning for me. The difference between him and God is that God is available, loves me unconditionally, and is patiently waiting for me to just return and respond to Him.

SHE SPOKE VOLUMES

You don't know what your words mean to her.

You don't know how they impact her attitude.

It's obvious that you don't know because of your behavior.

We know because when you broke your promise because we witnessed her in shambles.

We no longer want to clean up after the mess you make.

...AND THEN SOME

When she is quiet for long periods of time, do not celebrate too quickly. She may be thinking about her exit strategy or she may be reducing your influence and impact in her life or she may be thinking about someone else who she is wondering will love her more than you want to. Whatever the reason for her silence, there's certain to be some distance as a result. I just hope you don't need the distance formula to figure out how far away she is. Please keep her talking.

$$\sqrt{(x_2-x_1)^2 + (y_2-y_1)^2}$$

Silence speaks volumes.
You should keep her talking.

. . . AND THEN SOME

It is a shame that you need a grim reason to love authentically.

Don't continue to love small.

Love.

Love big!!!

Give it ALL that you have.

If you don't have any love, behave about love like you do anything else: by any means necessary.

SHE SPOKE VOLUMES

Just stop avoiding the opportunity of a great life.

'I'm in love with you'

are some of the most powerful words on the planet.

Use them more often!

Without fear!

Without consequence!

Without regret!!!

Without fear of hearing or not hearing them in return.

...AND THEN SOME

People don't avoid love because they don't know how. People avoid love because it costs. The fear overwhelms them and they decide to concede and let that fear be most important aspect, rather than participating in a beautiful experience called love.

SHE SPOKE VOLUMES

If the truth is not in your toolbox,
maybe you should stop talking until
it becomes available and useable.

. . . AND THEN SOME

WHY DO WE AVOID THE MOMENT OF TRUTH WHERE WE WALK INTO OUR DESTINY?

SHE SPOKE VOLUMES

The

incorrect

use

of

pronouns

can

cause

strife

within

your

relationships.

. . . AND THEN SOME

IT'S TRUE THAT I HAVE JUDGED YOU ON PAST AND PRESENT EXPERIENCES.

SHE SPOKE VOLUMES

The normal excuses are no longer effective.

Do your best!!!!

Stop letting yourself off of the hook.

...AND THEN SOME

Who are you when you love?

IF I STOP TALKING TO YOU THEN, I LIMIT THE NUMBER OF LIES YOU CAN TELL ME.

There is power when you show up. Milestones are achieved when you show up. People are blessed when you show up. Take time to show up. The investment to show up is worth the outcome of showing up. So, show up for yourself and others.

SHE SPOKE VOLUMES

WHAT EXACTLY HAPPENED THAT CAUSED YOU TO STOP DREAMING?

. . . AND THEN SOME

You

are

not

equipped

to

support

me

for

the

fight

I'm

in.

Thank you for resigning.

I accept.

SHE SPOKE VOLUMES

THERE'S NO REWARD FOR STEPPING ON SOMEONE ELSE'S DREAMS.

. . . AND THEN SOME

Being angry with God does not stop God from blessing you.

SHE SPOKE VOLUMES

I accepted you at face value.

That failed me.

Next time don't send your representative.

...AND THEN SOME

If you cannot afford for what you to say to be repeated, then you should strongly consider whether you should say it at all.

WHAT YOU SAID AND WHAT YOU MEANT TO SAY ARE EXTREMELY DIFFERENT.

LIKEWISE, WHAT I SAID AND WHAT YOU HEARD WERE DIFFERENT AS WELL.

. . . AND THEN SOME

I'M TRYING NOT TO FAIL THE TEST WHERE I'M SUPPOSED TO BE STILL AND LET HIM BE GOD.

SHE SPOKE VOLUMES

Why do we ask questions that we already know the answer to?

Is it so that the other party can redeem themselves?

Are we testing for the truth, truth we so desperately desire in another?

... AND THEN SOME[151] | GAGE

...AND THEN SOME

I will forever be amazed at your walk, your struggle, your overcoming, your spirit, your intellect, your stick-to-it-iveness, and your overwhelming love.

Don't quit.

HAPPY MOTHER'S DAY!!!!!!

SHE SPOKE VOLUMES

When I saw a picture of that 5-year-old girl, it arrested my attention.

When you look at the 5-year-old image of yourself, are you living the dreams of that 5-year-old?

If not, when will you start?

What will you do with that dream to start her reality?

. . . AND THEN SOME

Fierce,

authentic and

extravagant:

that's

how

I

want

my

love

defined.

SHE SPOKE VOLUMES

Every experience I have is designed to drive me back to God.

... AND THEN SOME

Please be careful what you place value on.

JUST A FRIENDLY REMINDER THAT THIS IS THE COMPUTER AGE. YOUR LIES AND "STORIES" CAN BE VERIFIED WHILE YOU ARE MAKING THEM UP WITH THE PHONE OR TABLET IN THE PALM MY HAND! THIS IS YOUR ONLY WARNING.

. . . AND THEN SOME

Stop

hoping

that

he

will

choose

you

because

God already did!

SHE SPOKE VOLUMES

Pray for all teachers!

We are chasing hearts and minds toward education, achievement and success.

. . . AND THEN SOME

When your spouse loses faith and can no longer pray,

I hope you are the first to know.

SHE SPOKE VOLUMES

Why

    are

        you

            living

                in the

                    alternative

                        zone

                            of

                                life?

                            Center stage is available.

. . . AND THEN SOME

What

are

you

going

to do

to

infuse

your

purpose

back

into

your

life?

SHE SPOKE VOLUMES

WHAT DID YOU DO TODAY TO HELP SOMEONE ELSE GROW?

. . . AND THEN SOME

I SEEM TO BE NOTORIOUS FOR LOVING YOU ABOVE YOUR MEANS.

SHE SPOKE VOLUMES

SOMETIMES LISTENING IS THE SOLUTION!

... AND THEN SOME[165] | GAGE

… AND THEN SOME

What's worth not quitting on?

SHE SPOKE VOLUMES

He did what he said he would without a single, solitary excuse.

...AND THEN SOME

Please get your LIE together!!!
Your story still has holes in it and
I'm about to expose it in its entirety
in just a second.

WHAT'S WRONG WITH MY TRUTH?

MY BEHAVIOR WAS IN RESPONSE TO WHAT YOU DID.

STOP DOING THAT WHICH CAUSES ME TO EXPOSE YOUR INAPPROPRIATE BEHAVIOR.

...AND THEN SOME

Relationships are dependent on all parties involved.

Please participate at the highest possible level.

If you can't participate at the highest level, just opt out.

SHE SPOKE VOLUMES

If

there

were

no

consequences

for

your

truth,

then

there

would

be

no

need

for

your

lies.

. . . AND THEN SOME[171] | GAGE

...AND THEN SOME

If it is impossible for me to be me when I'm with you, then I need to depart. I can't be your idea of me; that may change at any time and I may fail you, but I will definitely fail myself. I have to be myself.

SHE SPOKE VOLUMES

I
didn't
ask
you
because
I
didn't
believe
you
would
or
could.

. . . AND THEN SOME

God, Your words make my heart flutter.

SHE SPOKE VOLUMES

Anything worth having is worth working for!

I have challenged myself to follow my own advice in all possible areas. To support that, that means I will be doing some things that I have been intending to do but just haven't or have forgotten. At any rate, my advance apologies for the discomfort this may cause. Otherwise you are welcome to join me. If your advice is worth following, then you should be first!

SHE SPOKE VOLUMES

THERE'S NOTHING LIKE SOMEONE REMINDING YOU OF THE WORTH OF SOMETHING OR SOMEONE IN WHICH YOU ARE IN RELATIONSHIP.

. . . AND THEN SOME

Love has to be brave enough to say so and have those actions match. Love has enough power to bring another to their highest heights and to their lowest depths. Love has a passion that needs to be considered carefully. Do you know the actual power of your own love? Since you do not know that measure, then that means that you do not know the power of another's love either. The measure of passion is important. Love is the strength needed to move obstacles and delete hurdles. Love is how we got here. Not the love or the absence thereof related to your parents, but a real Love created you. His love is what created that passion that is inside of you that you desperately desire to share with others, especially one special other. Take extreme measures to love. The other person is waiting.

SHE SPOKE VOLUMES

Pull out your **dream** list & start

dreaming

again!

... AND THEN SOME[179] | GAGE

... AND THEN SOME

THE KIND OF LOVE WHICH WEATHERS STORMS. WHAT WE ALL DESIRE. AND DESERVE.

I vow to love you completely, authentically, and compassionately for the rest of our days.

All of the **14,620** days plus whatever else God's allows.

Without end, my love is real.

... AND THEN SOME

It was the type of goodbye that was definitive and spoke volumes, making one wonder if the word goodbye was powerful enough to be used.

SHE SPOKE VOLUMES

MAY THESE WORDS FALL ON FRESH EARS, AN OPEN MIND AND A WARM HEART. MAY THESE WORDS SOOTHE YOUR SOUL, REFRESHING YOU AND COMFORTING YOU.

...AND THEN SOME

Pray

with

a

BELIEVING

heart.

SHE SPOKE VOLUMES

WHAT IT COST YOU AND WHAT IT'S WORTH ARE TWO DIFFERENT MEASUREMENTS!

WHAT DO YOU HAVE TO SHOW FOR YOUR TIME SPENT?

... AND THEN SOME[185] | GAGE

...AND THEN SOME

Please name your children & your grandchildren names which are resume friendly, which will afford them an opportunity at the position rather than file 13, and so that other children will not ask them, "When your mother named you, was she on crack?" says the kid at the skate park.

> **RELATIONSHIPS ARE SACRED PLACES FOR WOMEN. PLEASE STOP CHEATING ON HER. JUST WALK AWAY SO SHE CAN HAVE SOME PERSONAL DIGNITY.**

SHE SPOKE VOLUMES

THIS THE CONTINUATION OF AN INCREDIBLE LIFE!

DREAM BIG AND WORK HARD!!!

SOME WORDS YOU CANNOT TAKE BACK!

... AND THEN SOME[187] | GAGE

...AND THEN SOME

Certain events recently have made me question if I have ever had a real man to love me other than God, my father, great-grandfather and grandfather. Love and 'in-love' is supposed to last longer than the last event that happened between two people. When I loved him, I thought it would last forever. Forever ended way earlier than expected and designed. I want to love authentically and freely, deeply and spiritually. I am waiting on my reveal, my man.

SHE SPOKE VOLUMES

Why are we always discouraged from saying what's really important?

People dislike fake people, but they despise real people because they challenge the fake.

Authenticity has a price.

#MostAuthenticPersonIKnow #247365

... AND THEN SOME[189] | GAGE

...AND THEN SOME

> You can't keep me over or under this barrel without God's consent and I'm about to be moved from that yoke!

BE IN THE MOMENT.
BE IN THE ROOM.

SHE SPOKE VOLUMES

I'm only able to teach what I know. So, when I ask you about your situation and I have great information, advice and resources, don't be surprised or amazed or confused. Just accept it. If it works for you, even consider paying me. But just don't discount it or look around.

...AND THEN SOME

I'm really tired of telling you what you should be doing and how you should be exercising your gifts. How long will you make God wait for your obedience?

satan uses whoever signs up, even at the church.

Don't ever criticize a woman who has tattered toe boxes on her shoes (the toe area). The absence of that leather or color is not because she can't take care of her shoes. It means that she cares more about prayer than shoe maintenance. Only praying women have this mark on their shoes. Go woman of God! Keep praying and eventually they will stop looking at your shoes and start understanding your prayers.

...AND THEN SOME

My kids are going to be exactly like me. Pray for the preacher's kids!

When you share something with someone, please do not be surprised if or when they repeat that. You gave them authorization to repeat the information when you shared it.

SHE SPOKE VOLUMES

GOD, YOU HAVE TRULY GIVEN satan ACCESS TO ME. I HOPE YOU TAKE IT BACK SOON.

There is a HUGE distance between what you want to do and what you are able to do, and an even bigger distance from what you are willing to do.

... AND THEN SOME

Some conversations should only happen when two people are standing face-to-face in a dark, empty bedroom.

I ask my daughter and son every day what did they learn in school today. Their answer breaks my heart. They say nothing or not much. I started asking myself at the end of the day, what did I learn today. From time to time, ask yourself what did you learn, who did you teach today, and was I intentional about learning today?

SHE SPOKE VOLUMES

Find someone to have faith in, invest in them, share how to believe, and watch God work.

"Love her beyond your means!"

The Intensive Retreat for Couples By Onedia N. Gage

...AND THEN SOME

It's been storming in my life for awhile. I thank God for the storm because it did not flood. I'm still here. I'm still gifted. I'm still loved. I'm still in His service. I'm still grateful and faithful.

On the negative side of the bell curve!

I was across enemy lines and didn't even know it. God protected me and provided for me and kept me as His own. It wasn't supposed to be the enemy's territory. You were supposed to love me. I had to take the scripture love your enemy to a whole new level.

...AND THEN SOME

Life needs sound effects. Make a worthwhile noise.

Because selective hearing is fashionable.

One or two events can change how you see and experience life.

If you are going to love, don't do it half-heartedly.

Give it all you have!

Do what you have to make it work!!!!

. . . AND THEN SOME

Be aware of those things that render you silent.

```
Cherish the opportunity to love.

Love to the fullest; giving of your whole self.

Love authentically.
```

SHE SPOKE VOLUMES

Love extravagantly.

IF I WANT TO MAKE THIS LIST, I MIGHT WANT TO GET STARTED.

... AND THEN SOME[203] | GAGE

...AND THEN SOME

The most powerful relationships overcome stuff!

Be an overcomer!

I'M GOING TO GET THIS RIGHT THIS TIME.

SHE SPOKE VOLUMES

When she said that she stopped existing and started living, I started to cry. I am still holding my handkerchief. Life is too short for foolishness. I am glad that she learned that as well.

I know that the fight I'm in is designed for me. I'm thankful to not have been picked for some other struggles. However, this has such a deep indescribable pain that I'm wondering how God will resolve it and heal me from my pain.

... AND THEN SOME

When we consider what's important and what's not, a lot should be eliminated! Today, decide to be the hero, champion, and inspiration that someone else needs to see so that they will be motivated to start a life they can be proud of and then they can overcome what stifles them.

I'm working harder this year so that I can wear the game changer title daily.

SHE SPOKE VOLUMES

If I don't die, I'll recover from this too.

STOP ACTING LIKE IT DOESN'T HURT.

IT DOES.

IT REALLY DOES.

. . . AND THEN SOME[207] | GAGE

When I made this look easy, that was an accident. I was not showing off or being arrogant. That effortless movement of my mind and hand was because of HOURS of effort and practice. I love what I do. I live out my passion.

SHE SPOKE VOLUMES

The severity of your situation is determined by the verbs you use.

WHEN YOU CONSIDER THE VALUE OF THE WORD OF GOD, PLEASE DISCONTINUE LISTENING WHEN YOU HAVE NO INTENTION OF DOING WHAT YOU HEARD.

... AND THEN SOME[209] | GAGE

. . . AND THEN SOME

I'm earning the opportunity to witness to women who are hurting and are bruised, who are broken and need support so that she does not quit!!!!! Don't bunt the ball. Swing for the fence!!!!!!

SHE SPOKE VOLUMES

Love is a Verb!

An action.

It's something you do.

Not something to do.

It requires your absolute engagement.

Not something you talk about.

Not something you think about.

Not something you get around to.

Not something you muse about.

Not even something you dream.

If can't do it, then keep your hands to yourself.

The damage is too heavy.

The number of persons hurt is too numerous.

The number of opportunities is too few.

None of which should be affected because of your lack of self-control.

. . . AND THEN SOME

every day matters!

every moment counts!

pursue what you love with all that you have!

You need more than a point of tangency to build a successful relationship.

SHE SPOKE VOLUMES

THE KIND OF LOVE WHICH WEATHERS STORMS.

WHAT WE ALL DESIRE.

AND DESERVE.

THERE IS EXTREME VALUE IN UNANTICIPATED LOVE.

... AND THEN SOME[213] | GAGE

...AND THEN SOME

That hurt and you cannot take it back!

SOME MISTAKES SHOULD NOT BE MADE TWICE!

ONCE WAS ACTUALLY TOO MANY.

SHE SPOKE VOLUMES

"There is a sacredness in tears. They are not the mark of weakness but of power. They are messengers of overwhelming grief and of unspeakable love." Washington Irving. So, when you see my tears be careful of what happens next. Be prepared to be amazed and overwhelmed, surprised and educated.

WERE YOU LISTENING?

DID YOU HEAR WHAT SHE JUST SAID?

...AND THEN SOME

Stop finding reasons to underachieve, be mediocre, to avoid your propose, and be accountable for your destiny. I promise that flying under the radar scheme is much more time consuming than doing what you are supposed to be doing, fulfilling God's purpose, and truly joyful.

… AND THEN SOME | GAGE

YOUR LIFE IS A LOVE STORY!

Hannah's words just got personal.

1 Samuel 1 & 2.

...AND THEN SOME

I'm at my maximum capacity for foolishness. God please rescue now.

It's like repeating the same lesson over and over with the same outcome.

Get off the merry go round.

SHE SPOKE VOLUMES

LOVE AND PRIDE DO NOT EXIST IN THE SAME SPACE.

IT'S HARD TO FIGHT FOR WHAT DOES NOT BELONG TO YOU.

. . . AND THEN SOME

When I said the opposite of love was hate, he corrected me and said that the opposite of love was indifference. I stepped back, and corrected my statement. I realized that not only was he right, he was also brave. What happened next was the real problem: my indifference was too loud, too intense, too intentional and too permanent.

When I love, I LOVE.

When I don't, you know it.

SHE SPOKE VOLUMES

Who makes you better?

Who challenges you to achieve?

To succeed?

To try harder?

To overcome?

. . . AND THEN SOME

Newton's Laws of Physics: An object at rest stays at rest and an object in motion stays in motion with the same speed and in the same direction unless acted upon by an unbalanced force. According to Newton, an object will only accelerate if there is a net or unbalanced force acting upon it. For every action, there is an equal and opposite reaction.

When you consider your relationships, could you use these laws to move your relationship along? To the best possible place? What does it take to move your relationship forward?

SHE SPOKE VOLUMES

What will you do because of the love you have for another person?

Pursue your dreams. Start anywhere. Just start!

I want to give you the courage to live out loud!

... AND THEN SOME[223] | GAGE

. . . AND THEN SOME

When you pick a fight, pick one which leads you to loving another person greater than you ever thought possible, better than they think they deserve, and more extravagantly than is even reasonable. Life is too short for anything else. You deserved to be loved at that level and you deserve to love at that same level of extravagance!

SHE SPOKE VOLUMES

Is this what it looks like to love me?

Please do not be hard to love. Make it easy to love you.

...AND THEN SOME[225] | GAGE

...AND THEN SOME

You are equipped for the fight you are in.

I HAVE LOTS TO TEACH YOU, SO PLEASE GET PREPARED TO LEARN. TAKE OUT A WRITING INSTRUMENT, SOME PAPER, AND CLEAR YOUR HEART. THIS LESSON IS RIGOROUS, TIMELY, TIME SENSITIVE, AND NECESSARY.

SHE SPOKE VOLUMES

The kind of love that makes you come home at night.

The muse of love that offers you peace and contentment.

A love that craves and consoles.

...AND THEN SOME

do you remember when you understood the power of

prayer?

When you act like that young person is not

disposable,

but has **value**,

then you have done your job!

SHE SPOKE VOLUMES

When

you

start

living

as if

tomorrow

is a

guarantee,

you

have

already

committed

the

worst

of

errors.

. . . AND THEN SOME

Cherish the opportunity to love.

Love to the fullest;

Giving of your whole self.

Love authentically.

Love extravagantly.

SHE SPOKE VOLUMES

We need to stop feeling like we are somebody or have accomplished something because "they" stamp our work with that award.

#sendamessage #stopofferingthemtheopportunitytosayno #ourownawardsshow #denzelishisowndude #doitforthepowerofthework #stopmakingbootlegdvds

...AND THEN SOME

When you are ready to love, you will make yourself available.

I AM GLAD MY HEART IS NOT HARD. I CAN LOVE FREELY. I CAN FORGIVE. I CAN TRUST. I CAN BELIEVE.

SHE SPOKE VOLUMES

A woman may not know if/when a man loves her, but she certainly knows when he doesn't.

Please check me if I treat other Christians terribly while we are standing in church. I just experienced it and I'm impressed by my lack of response. It's not the first time from the same person. Not sure how long my non-response will continue.

... AND THEN SOME[233] | GAGE

... AND THEN SOME

SILENCE SPEAKS VOLUMES.

WHEN I AM SILENT, I AM STILL COMMUNICATING.

YOU JUST MAY NOT LIKE THE MESSAGE.

SHE SPOKE VOLUMES

Fall in love with the highest image of yourself.

Do not authorize the demise of your already wilted self-esteem.

Others already want to see your fail.

Set them aside, figure out who you are, live through your own vision and upgrade your self-portrait.

... AND THEN SOME

YOU SHOULD BE EAGER TO SHUT YOUR OWN EXCUSES DOWN.

Some of the most important and powerful and profound remarks can be said in under a minute.

SHE SPOKE VOLUMES

I need to hear more from you.

I need to hear from you louder and more intimately.

It is prudent to understand yourself so that the other person has a chance to do the same.

. . . AND THEN SOME

Caution: this level is critical for your next!

"Tell me what you know good." Sam Gage, Jr. He asked every day and waited for an answer. I learned to be prepared to answer because the advice which followed was priceless.

SHE SPOKE VOLUMES

IF YOU REPLAY THAT HURT IN YOUR MIND, IN YOUR HEART, OR ALOUD, THAT HURT SEEMS REAL, AND NEW, WHICH MAKES FORGIVENESS AND HEALING IMPOSSIBLE. STOP RETELLING THAT STORY OF HOW HE LEFT YOU, HOW SHE CHEATED, HOW YOU DID MORE THAN THE OTHER PERSON, AND WHATEVER ELSE YOUR STORY. YOUR STORY IS VALUABLE FOR HEALING AND OVERCOMING, MOTIVATION AND EXCELLING. NOT FOR REVENGE OR REGRET.

. . . AND THEN SOME

What do you when your voice shuts down the voices of those around you, but they deserve to be heard?

The valley is where the work is done.

SHE SPOKE VOLUMES

You only have to win by one point to be the winner!

Stop trying to justify the loss or the win, for that matter.

When we said let Him use you, we meant God, Jesus and the Holy Spirit. Nobody else.

... AND THEN SOME

Be a better person when 'dumb and stupid' present itself. Be a better co-parent than you were a mate. Your pettiness throws shade on you; not the person you were trying hurt and harm because of your pre-existing bitter condition.

SHE SPOKE VOLUMES

I

didn't

praise

God

because

you

were

watching.

I

worship

because

I

needed

to get

God's

attention!

. . . AND THEN SOME

Lack of action sends a stronger message.

And one you may not have anticipated.

Causing a response that you were not ready for.

---

image.

value.

self-worth.

self-respect.

love is rare.

people are in relationships for way more reasons other than love.

IF YOUR HEART IS GOING TO ACHE AS A RESULT OF YOUR LACK OF ACTION,

THEN YOU MAY WANT TO RECONSIDER KEEPING QUIET.

... AND THEN SOME

Manage to make the space she shares with you the first place where she feels totally comfortable being herself.

Love.

Are you the definition and the demonstration?

SHE SPOKE VOLUMES

If you are willing and able to put in the work, then you can have the title and the position. Not before.

Relationship minefields: how many secrets do you have? That is the same number your mate can have. Good luck on that very unsuccessful adventure.

...AND THEN SOME

Don't let others disbelieve you.

It causes you to disbelieve too.

You cannot have an extraordinary life walking with an ordinary attitude.

Your life is a love story!

Be worth the effort others exert for you.

...AND THEN SOME

Just so that you are clear and because I hope you will foster the opportunity to do the same: I protect my heart with a subjective fierceness that may seem over the top. I am sure that my methods seem too intense however, I cannot afford the destruction which is bound to be the result of my heart being in the wrong hands. So, if you are not sure you are ready to handle my heart carefully and most judiciously, please stay in place until the Storm (me) comes to a complete stop. You would be better off and most benefitted to stay in your position, shelter in place, and let the Storm (me) pass by.

SHE SPOKE VOLUMES

If I cannot be 'all in,' a poker announcement when you push all of your chips to the middle of the table and the verbal and matching announcement, "I am all in!", then I am out. This move means that your hand of cards is worth your total investment, so I am saying the same: my heart and yours is worth the TOTAL INVESTMENT. If that announcement and behavior scares or scars you, then you should just keep admiring me from the same distance you have been admiring me from. I cannot and will not love you at that distance or under those conditions.

. . . AND THEN SOME[251] | GAGE

...AND THEN SOME

My heart is tender and precious and does not need any damage. I love with power and intensity, respect and honor, admiration and adoration. So, there are requirements and standards, which will be upheld or an immediate dismissal will result.

SHE SPOKE VOLUMES

THERE IS ALWAYS THE POSSIBILITY THAT SOMEONE HAD EXPECTATIONS OF YOU WITH WHICH THEY WILL NEVER SHARE.

What have you settled for today? Was it worth it?

... AND THEN SOME[253] | GAGE

. . . AND THEN SOME

Sometimes silence says more than words.

One look defines some extremely powerful moments.

Take extreme measures to love.

The other person is waiting.

Two women cannot occupy the same heart.

Mediocrity is a place of misunderstood comfort. It is a dangerous place to frequent. We might mistake it for an okay place to reside mentally, spiritually, and physically. Move out of the mediocrity. Greatness is available and is waiting.

...AND THEN SOME

Women, remember we have gotten to some very amazing places and become very amazing women because of another woman's sacrifice. Don't make her look bad or regret that sacrifice because of your bad decisions and poor behavior.

Until I stop forgiving you.

Until I stop wanting you.

Until I stop loving you, I'll be right here.

SHE SPOKE VOLUMES

No more excuses.

LOVE IS BEAUTIFUL WHEN BOTH PARTIES PARTICIPATE!

...AND THEN SOME

Who you want me to be is different from who I am.

The disappointment is that I'm better than you want me to be.

When you specialize in ignorance, you are sure to arrive there!

SHE SPOKE VOLUMES

WHEN THE PAIN IS BIG ENOUGH, WE TAKE THE BEST ACTIONS.

The fight you just picked was meant to last awhile but I only have it scheduled for 15 minutes. And your time is just about up!!!!

... AND THEN SOME[259] | GAGE

...AND THEN SOME

"I want us." Alone those words mean nothing. Together they change lives. Work hard for "us."

Each day without excuse and without shame.

You cannot expect big results with low effort. You have to give big to get big! GO BIG! So many people want something(s) but do want to exert any energy to provoke those results. Get to work!

SHE SPOKE VOLUMES

Please tell me the WHOLE story. Give me the details. Let me decide for myself. Do not take any short cuts. Do not assume I know anything. Especially about your situation. I deserve to know the details. So, I can decide what is best for me.

When a person acts like they have nothing to live for, be really careful. There is a difference between expanding the limits and boundaries versus abandoning them altogether.

. . . AND THEN SOME

you have the power through encouragement and belief to help lift another out of their own, maybe self-inflicted, emotional abyss.

show up in someone's life.

today.

ANY OLD EXCUSE WILL DO.

SHE SPOKE VOLUMES

And you survived, and you had no idea you would. And you healed in ways you thought you never would. And you can smile and hold your head up because God is there, and He is the strength in your jaws and your cheekbones to smile.

Onedia N. Gage Excerpt from WITH AN ANOINTED VOICE

. . . AND THEN SOME

I think you just asked me to audition for the lead role but there is not an existing position in your life. I am not working for a job which does not exist in hopes that I will do so well that a position will be created for me. I think you have love confused with corporate America.

DID IT EVER OCCUR TO YOU THAT HER DRY RESPONSE WAS A COVER FOR HER HURT AND POSSIBLE PAIN BECAUSE SHE SUBMITTED TO UNFORESEEN FOOLISHNESS!!!!!

SHE SPOKE VOLUMES

Mediocrity is a place of misunderstood comfort. It is a dangerous place to frequent. We might mistake it for an okay place to reside mentally, spiritually, and physically. Move out of the mediocrity. Greatness is available and is waiting.

When I witness your worship, you become so much more attractive to me.

. . . AND THEN SOME

I roused myself and you were often just as an audience.

I know that this is arrogant, but true.

I never covered your failures or shortcomings.

I understand now how I added to your pain.

SHE SPOKE VOLUMES

You don't have to be demonstrative to be compassionate; but it certainly is more powerful.

YESTERDAY'S LOVE DOES NOT COUNT

...AND THEN SOME

You are ignorant to my pain;

You are oblivious to my needs;

You are closed to *my* voice;

You are blind to my tears.

SHE SPOKE VOLUMES

> *I'm used to people not loving me. You are not doing anything new.*

... AND THEN SOME

It is a privilege to live your life out loud. You should do it more often.

FIND OUT WHAT MAKES YOU HAPPY. START DOING THAT RIGHT NOW.

SHE SPOKE VOLUMES

It was good enough when we used it to raise you!

When you are tired of mediocrity, you will do something differently. It will be different simply because you made a decision. Stop listening to the noise no matter how close it is.

... AND THEN SOME

Everyone knows someone who is fake. Stop letting it be you.

Are you prepared to give over all of the TOOLS necessary for the other person to be successful in a relationship with you? If not, stop! Stop engaging in relationships! Most of us are not ready to be transparent enough to share with others. So just STOP!! Please!

SHE SPOKE VOLUMES

Authentic

love

is

intentional.

. . . AND THEN SOME

When you pick a fight, pick one which leads you to loving another person greater than you ever thought possible, better than they think they deserve, and more extravagantly than is even reasonable. Life is too short for anything else. You deserve to love at that level and you deserve to be loved at that same level of extravagance!

SHE SPOKE VOLUMES

SHARE YOUR REAL HEART . . . UNLESS YOU HAVEN'T SEEN IT OR HEARD FROM IT OR FELT IT OR TRUSTED IT IN A WHILE.

. . . AND THEN SOME

EVEN DAVID HAD TO FIGHT.

YOU ARE NOT ANY DIFFERENT AND CERTAINLY NOT BETTER THAN.

JUST FIGHT.

EVEN THOUGH YOU DO NOT WANT TO.

GOD ALREADY HAS PREPARED THE BATTLE PLAN,

THE BATTLE FIELD AND A MIND READY FOR BATTLE.

Be compassionate to others. Treat them like you want to be treated—better than we all deserve. Do it all day, today. Then, do it every day. Look into their eyes to see what they need, then give it to them. It will help you to be well within your soul.

. . . AND THEN SOME

if I could marry my best friend....
someone I am already transparent with.
someone whose motives I am not ever questioning.
someone who has already heard me cry so it does not catch him by surprise.
someone who loves me because I am sexy in the morning.
someone who tries to pay attention to my ambition.
someone who will tell me the truth when the dress makes my butt look big and says let's go, you look great.
or finds me something else to wear.
someone who understands that I am comfortable in his sweats and t-shirts at home.
and understand that I will fall asleep during my own team's football game and because I do not snore it is okay.
And he tells me who won when I wake up.
someone who eats the food that I cook.
understands when I don't.
and loves whatever I bake.
and tells me his favorite stuff.
understands how to be surprised in a good way: gifts, notes, poetry.
someone who reads my works and asks enough questions or offers enough feedback to be considered engaged and invested and helpful.
Someone who prays for me--in private and in my presence.
The man who understands the outlandish and outrageous pursuit of my heart and mind, my spirit and soul.

If I could marry my best friend.

PERFECT WORDS

By Onedia N. Gage, Ph. D.

Finding the words escape me
Perfect ones impossible
Words meaning too much
Yet not quite enough
To describe the unthinkable
The indescribable

Imagine what words evolve
Describing the soul's depth
Love's adventures
Sadness
Life's desires
Dreams deferred
Fear

If only I could master the
Perfect words
Describing my soul's depth
My heart's matters
My mind's thoughts

Then and only when will you
Hear the perfect words
For which I seek to speak

If I could be true to you about my feelings

...AND THEN SOME

And truer still about my words
Would I draw you closer
Or move you from my person
Completely

The difficulty lies in finding the

Perfect Words.

ACKNOWLEDGEMENTS

God, thank You for Your plans for me. Thank You for ***She Spoke Volumes . . . And Then Some*** and choosing me to complete Your project with the words that come out of my mouth. I just want to please You. Thank You for continuing to anoint me and to invest in me and my gifts, which keep surprising me. Thank You for loving and forgiving me.

Hillary and Nehemiah, thank you for supporting me and my endeavors. Thank you for loving me, especially when I do nothing without a pen and a clipboard, thank you for enduring my late nights, your ideas, the sounding board, the love and the support. Thank you for celebrating our legacy.

To my prayer partners and to my accountability partners, thank you for the long talks and the powerful prayers and the encouragement. To my pastor and church family, thank you so much for your love and support.

. . . AND THEN SOME

Onedia N. Gage speaks volumes. Sometimes no one is listening. Other times people cannot listen enough. But what she says is quite powerful. Timely. Judicious. Poignant. Insightful. Direct. Authentic. True.

Please feel free to contact and share your feedback, onediagage@onediagagespeaks.com, or @onediangage (twitter). www.onediagagespeaks.com
Blogtalkradio.com/onediagage
Youtube.com/onediagage10
Facebook.com/onedia-gage

. . . AND THEN SOME

SHE SPOKE VOLUMES

CONFERENCE SPEAKER ♦ WORKSHOP LEADER

To invite Dr. Gage to speak at your event,

Please contact us at: www.onedigagespeaks.com

@onediangage (twitter) ♦ onediagage@onediagagespeaks.com ♦ facebook.com/onediagage

youtube.com/onediagage ♦ blogtalkradio.com/onediagage ♦ ongage (Instagram)

… AND THEN SOME

Publishing

Do you have a book you want to write, but do not know what to do?
Do you have a book you need to publish but do not know how to start?
Would publishing move your career forward?

Let us help

onediagage@purpleink.net ♦ www.purpleink.net

281.740.5143 ♦ 512.715.4243

www.ingramcontent.com/pod-product-compliance
Lightning Source LLC
Chambersburg PA
CBHW081345080526
44588CB00016B/2385